The Full Sufficiency of Christ

Explaining the gospel for both the new believer and questioning seeker

By Christopher Hearn

Front and back cover artwork by Gijo Tirado. www.GijoDesign.com.

Unless otherwise indicated, all Scripture quotations are from The Holy Bible, English Standard Version® (ESV®), copyright © 2001 by Crossway, a publishing ministry of Good News Publishers. Used by permission. All rights reserved.

The Scripture quotation marked (NIV) is All Scripture quotations, in this publication are from the HOLY BIBLE, NEW INTERNATIONAL VERSION® NIV® Copyright © 1973, 1978, 1984, 2011 by Biblica, Inc.®. Used by permission. All rights reserved worldwide.

Copyright © 2013 Christopher Hearn
All rights reserved.
ISBN: ISBN-13: 978-1494461775
ISBN-10: 1494461773

Dedication

Thank you to Stacey Batista, Chris Platt and Dr. Mark Strauss for help reviewing the manuscript. To my Dad, Bob Hearn, for the many email discussions on some of the topics covered in this book.

Also to Linda Roberts for style editing and to Gijo Tirado for a super job with the front and back covers. Gravitas!

"For he has rescued us from the dominion of darkness and brought us into the kingdom of the Son he loves, in whom we have redemption, the forgiveness of sins" (Colossians 1:13-14. NIV).

Contents

Introduction	7
1 What is sin?	9
2 Can my being a good person get me into Heaven?	13
3 What is the gospel and what does it mean to believe in the gospel?	19
4 Why did Jesus have to die?	23
5 Why did Jesus have to be God?	29
6 Why did Jesus have to rise from the dead?	35
7 Why is faith in Jesus the only way to know God?	39
8 Why do people go to Hell?	43
9 How can I personally know God?	49

Appendix

A Do I have to be baptized in order to go to Heaven?	51
B What about James, chapter 2?	55
C Does Purgatory exist?	59
D Poem- The Thief on the Cross	65
E Poem- Jesus is always with me	67

Introduction

Why did Jesus have to die for me to be forgiven by God?
What does it mean when the Bible says that I'm a sinner?
Why do people go to Hell if God is a God of love?
Is Jesus the only way to know God and go to Heaven?
Can't I get to Heaven by living a good life?
Does God want everyone to go to Heaven?

Have you ever been asked one of these questions by a friend, coworker, or relative who was looking into Christianity? Maybe you've asked one of them these people yourself and have yet to find a satisfying answer. Perhaps you wouldn't call yourself a Christian, but you are reading about Christianity and have asked one of these questions yourself. If so, then I'm glad you've taken some time out of your busy schedule to read this book.

I hope to answer these and other questions that are shared by both new Christians and those who are earnestly investigating Christianity. We'll dig deep, looking not only at the "what" but at the "why" as well.

8

1

WHAT IS SIN?

"For God so loved the world, that he gave his only Son, that whoever believes in him should not perish but have eternal life" (John 3:16).

Here it is, the classic verse. It's known in various languages around the world and gives hope and comfort to many. It tells us of God's incredible love for all humanity. And yes, that includes you.

But it brings to mind a few questions: "Why did God give His only Son? Why should I perish? Why do I have to believe in Jesus to have eternal life?"

These are some of the questions that we'll be looking at together in this book. We'll start out by taking a look at what is wrong with humanity, and then we'll move on to the one solution to our problem.

This means starting with the bad news. But just as a doctor needs to diagnose the illness in order to prescribe the correct cure, we need to look at humanity's illness first in order to see the way to health.

If we are honest with ourselves, we know that we make mistakes in life and that we do bad things. We have evil thoughts, we're prideful, we lie, we steal, we don't always treat others the way that we would like to be treated, and the list goes on from there. The Bible calls this sin.

Jill Carattini is managing editor of *A Slice of Infinity* at Ravi Zacharias International Ministries in Atlanta, Georgia. She writes,

> Great minds from Augustine to G. K. Chesterton saw clearly that the most verifiable truth of the Christian worldview is certainly the depravity of humanity. It can be observed across countries and languages, at any time and within every decade, from barbaric accounts of depravity in far away places to more accepted forms of depravity close at home.

We close our eyes to reality where we refuse to see the same story repeating itself again and again. We might euphemize the thought of sin into neurotic myth, outdated opinion, or church propaganda, but it has not been euthanized.[1]

The Bible teaches that people are sinners by nature and that we choose to sin or do wrong. As Romans says, "...all, both Jews and Greeks, are under sin, as it is written: "None is righteous, no, not one; no one understands; no one seeks for God. All have turned aside; together they have become worthless; no one does good, not even one...There is no fear of God before their eyes...there is no distinction: for all have sinned and fall short of the glory of God" (Romans 3:10–12, 3:18, 3:22b–23).

Without God, we're in bondage to sin. We're in chains. As Paul writes in Ephesians 2:3, "...we all once lived in the passions of our flesh, carrying out the desires of the body and the mind, and were by nature children of wrath, like the rest of mankind."

Also, the Bible teaches us that the good that we should do, but do not do, is sin as well: "...whoever knows the right thing to do and fails to do it, for him it is sin" (James 4:17).

The Bible says that our wrongdoings are primarily against God. Our sin is rebellion and disobedience directly against Him. When we sin, we are saying that we want to do things our way rather than God's way.

In Psalm 51:4, David says, "Against you, you only, have I sinned and done what is evil in your sight."

This is what David wrote after his sins concerning Bathsheba and Uriah were found out. Although his sins were against them, ultimately they were against God.

Being sinners also means that we are God's enemies. We may not see ourselves as being actively against God or as being one of His enemies, yet this is our relationship to God when we don't believe in Him.

In Romans 5:10, it says, "...while we were enemies we were reconciled to God by the death of his Son."

---

[1] Jill Carattini, "The Best Intentions," *A Slice of Infinity*. http://us5.campaign-archive2.com/?u=45b75085e6ab57e339ea89d67&id=948f6ba7ec&e=52eb9e4aa0

In fact, sin in its worst form is not believing in God, as exemplified by rejecting God by saying that He doesn't exist.

Our sin has an adverse effect on our relationships with God, and this carries over into how we act with others—and even to how we see ourselves.

How does our sin affect our relationships with God?

An apt word that comes to mind when considering sin is "separation." Our sin separates us from God.

In Isaiah 59:1–2, Isaiah says, "Behold, the Lord's hand is not shortened, that it cannot save, or his ear dull, that it cannot hear; but your iniquities have made a separation between you and your God, and your sins have hidden his face from you so that he does not hear."

Being separated from God has been described in many ways, such as trying to swim across the Atlantic Ocean to reach God, or jumping off the edge of the Grand Canyon to reach Him on the other side. In other words, anything that is impossible for us to do.

We could say that our condition before we come to know God is like that of one living in a house with a dangerously high level of carbon monoxide, but is completely unaware of it. That person's house does not have a detector.

Carbon monoxide is an odorless, tasteless, invisible gas. So you can't smell it, taste it, or see it. Therefore, while it would be pretty easy to dismiss any possible threats from carbon monoxide in the home, it wouldn't change the reality of the gas's presence.

It is similar with sin. You can say that you aren't a sinner and don't need God, and you can go right on living. In the same way, you may say that the threat from carbon monoxide in a home isn't real. But according to the *Journal of the American Medical Association*, carbon monoxide poisoning is the leading cause of accidental poisoning deaths in America.[2]

When one is poisoned by carbon monoxide, "The result is that the body becomes oxygen-starved, which can result in tissue damage and death."[3]

If we equate oxygen to God, then just as the body needs oxygen to live, so our souls need God to keep alive. Too much carbon monoxide keeps oxygen from the body, and in the same way, our sins keep us from God.

---

[2] The Ohio Home Inspections Company. "Carbon Monoxide." www.thehome-inspection.com/carbonmonoxide.htm
[3] Ibid.

We separate ourselves from God through our sinning and by our sinful natures. Our sin separates us from God because He is perfectly holy and righteous. He is also perfectly just, and His justice demands punishment when an offense, or sin, is committed against Him. Just as there are fines to pay for breaking the law, there is also a fine for breaking God's law, which is what we break when we sin against Him. The fine for our sin is death.

Sin in its very nature is death. James 1:15 says, "...sin when it is fully grown brings forth death."

Because sin is ultimately death, the Bible states that "...the wages of sin is death." (Romans 6:23).

The Bible teaches that there are two kinds of death. Both of them deal with separation. One type of death is the separation of our souls from our bodies (physical death). The other is the separation of God from ourselves (spiritual death).

We see Jesus talking about these two types of death in John 11:25–26, where He says, "I am the resurrection and the life. Whoever believes in me, though he die, yet shall he live, and everyone who lives and believes in me shall never die. Do you believe this?"

What Jesus is saying is that if anyone believes in Him, even though he or she will die physically, that person will live spiritually. That person will have eternal life with God in Heaven and will never die spiritually.

God, by nature, is eternal, and since our sins transgress or violate His very nature, the penalty for our sins is eternal death. In other words, the punishment is to be forever separated from the conscious presence of God and all of His blessings. This is what Hell is.

The bad news about sin and what it means in our relationships with the Lord may strike some as being unfair. But consider that all people willfully sin. I do. You do. Everyone does every day. We know that it would be impossible for anyone people to live every second of every day for the rest of their lives without sinning.

Our sin and sinful natures present all humanity with three main problems:

1. The penalty for our sins must be paid somehow by someone.
2. Our sinful natures need to change.
3. The separation between God and ourselves that is caused by our sin must somehow be bridged.

As we continue, we'll see how Jesus' death and resurrection solves all three of these problems for everyone who believes in Him.

2

CAN MY BEING A GOOD PERSON GET ME INTO HEAVEN?

Most of the world's religions, except for Christianity, teach that a mixture of faith and works is needed to be made right with God. While it is a popular idea, it is not correct.

It is impossible to perform enough good works or religious rituals in order to be accepted by God and allowed into Heaven. For one, God's standard of righteousness is 100 percent perfection, 100 percent of the time in thought, word, and deed. No one can keep that up for very long. Further, no matter how good we are in our lives, we still have our sinful natures, which keep us separated from the Lord.

Christianity is the only world religion that adequately deals with the three problems mentioned at the end of the last chapter: penalty, sinful nature, and separation. Only Christianity is based on God's grace and our faith in what He has done for us in order to bridge that separation and bring us to Him.

Scripture is clear in saying that we are saved by grace and not our own good works.

Ephesians 2:8–9 declares, "For by grace you have been saved through faith. And this is not your own doing; it is the gift of God, not a result of works, so that no one may boast."

Salvation is a free gift from God. It cannot be obtained by good works, baptism, church membership, church attendance, witnessing to others by knocking on doors, mission trips, or giving financially to a church.

For example, we all know from having birthday parties that we don't do anything to receive a birthday gift. You expect your friends to give your presents on your birthday. You don't have to go out and shovel out their driveway to earn your birthday present. You don't have to fix a person's leaky faucet, or do some other kind of favor for that person before he or she will give you your present. It is a free gift.

If salvation was earned, then it wouldn't be "the gift of God." It would be "the wages of God." We work in order to earn something. But Scripture says that "...the free gift of God is eternal life in Christ Jesus our Lord" (Romans 6:23).

The Bible also says in Romans 4:4–5, "Now to the one who works, his wages are not counted as a gift but as his due. And to the one who does not work but believes in him who justifies the ungodly, his faith is counted as righteousness."

Grace stands in opposition to works. Grace is us, as sinners, getting what we do not deserve (salvation) as a free gift. It's God's grace. It's His love and mercy in action, shown supremely by Jesus' death on the cross.

Grace means that salvation can be received by anyone at any place at any time. Grace means that deathbed conversions can happen. There is even a biblical example of a deathbed conversion: the thief on the cross next to Jesus.

In the Gospel of Luke, it says,
> One of the criminals who were hanged railed at him, saying, "'Are you not the Christ? Save yourself and us!'" But the other rebuked him, saying, "'Do you not fear God, since you are under the same sentence of condemnation? And we indeed justly, for we are receiving the due reward of our deeds; but this man has done nothing wrong.'" And he said, "'Jesus, remember me when you come into your kingdom.'" And he said to him, "Truly, I say to you, today you will be with me in Paradise." (Luke 23:39–43)

This man was saved (or entered into a personal relationship with God) and went to Heaven, even though he didn't do any of the following:

He didn't perform any acts of penance.
He couldn't be baptized.
He couldn't attend synagogue services or be made a member of the synagogue.
He couldn't get a seminary degree.
He couldn't do a single good work to make up for the bad he had done in his life.
He couldn't give any money to the temple treasury.

So what could he do? To most of the world, his eternal state would appear hopeless. This is obviously a person going to Hell with no U-turn in sight, right? And yet, there was one thing that he could do. Ironically, it is the only thing that anyone can do to enter into a personal relationship with God and go to Heaven. That is, he repented of his sins and believed in Jesus Christ.

Before he repented, the thief on the cross was a perfect example of humanity in its most helpless state before a holy and righteous God. He could do no good works to save himself.

And yet, Jesus welcomed him into His Kingdom. Not for just a tour or a little walk around, but for all eternity. That's grace.

God's grace means that anyone who believes in the deity of Jesus Christ and in the life, death, and bodily resurrection of Jesus as full payment for his or her sins goes to Heaven.

It doesn't matter what your background is, where you live, or the bad things that you've done. Literally, anyone in the world who believes the gospel will be saved.

Romans 10:9-11 says, "...if you confess with your mouth that Jesus is Lord and believe in your heart that God raised him from the dead, you will be saved. For with the heart one believes and is justified, and with the mouth one confesses and is saved. For the Scripture says, 'Everyone who believes in him will not be put to shame.'"

God's grace liberates us from the bondage of legalism. Legalism is a way to try to earn or merit God's love and approval through good works. If you aren't doing a lot of good in your life, you will have a constant fear that God won't love you. Legalism is very cruel to whomever is under its bondage. For the more a person tries to do good works and perform religious rituals to please God, the more inadequate he or she feels. That person may feel like he or she is failing God. So, the person tries to do more in hopes that he or she will be found "good enough," trying to reach some imaginary goal in his or her mind. But that person can never reach that goal, and the vicious cycle continues on, leading to more despair.

Soon after I entered a Christian college, I fell into the trap of legalism. I once told a friend of mine that I wanted to go to church to make sure that "it would count."

I have to admit that even at the time, I really didn't know what I was talking about. How would it count? What would it count for? I guess I had hoped to gain brownie points with God.

Yet, the truth is that God's love for us is always at maximum. No matter how you live, or what you do, He will never love you any less.

The Bible says that God is love. (1 John 4:8, 4:16)

You may say that you're too much of a sinner to be accepted by God. You've sinned too much. You've gone too far. But this isn't true.

Romans 5:8 says, "but God shows his love for us in that while we were still sinners, Christ died for us."

Paul in the above verse doesn't go into all of the various sins that one can commit against the Lord. He simply says that God loved us even when we were sinners. That includes any kind of sin committed any number of times.

Take, for example, the aforementioned thief on the cross. Remember that there was nothing particularly lovable about him; he himself admitted to being guilty of a crime worthy of death. Yet, Jesus accepted him into His Kingdom.

It may help for us to ask this question, "Which heart are we looking into? Ours or Gods?"

For if we are looking into our hearts and being honest, then there are a lot of reasons we can find to explain why God would not want to love us. But if we look into God's heart, all of those reasons simply melt away. For God's love for each one of us is based on His nature and not on what we do. This also defines grace; God giving us what we don't deserve. No matter what you think, feel, say, or do, God loves you as much as if you were perfect. He can't love you any more than He does right now. That's a powerful thought, isn't it? Even when we sin and blow it, or when we reject God outright, still He loves us and wants the best for us. God loves the vilest of sinners and the holiest of saints equally.

This is true because His love isn't centered in us. It comes from His nature. His love for us is rooted in Himself, not in ourselves or in or our actions. God is love, His nature is love, and therefore He can do nothing but love. All He does is love. He is free to act as He chooses, but when He does act, it can only be in full, total, and complete love.

God's grace has often been seen as a courtroom where God is the judge who says that we are sinners guilty of violating His Law and nature. We are guilty, and we know it. It is a hopeless scene. Then the Judge takes off His robes and stands in our place. He says that He will take our due punishment upon Himself. We are free, and Christ becomes guilty for our sins.

The Bible says in John 3:16–17, "For God so loved the world, that he gave his only Son, that whoever believes in him should not perish but have eternal life. For God did not send his Son into the world to condemn the world, but in order that the world might be saved through him."

2 Timothy 1:9 declares that God "saved us and called us to a holy calling, not because of our works but because of his own purpose and grace, which he gave us in Christ Jesus before the ages began."

Paul in Romans 9:30–10:4 writes,
> What shall we say, then? That Gentiles who did not pursue righteousness have attained it, that is, a righteousness that is by faith;
>
> but that Israel who pursued a law that would lead to righteousness did not succeed in reaching that law. Why? Because they did not pursue it by faith, but as if it were based on works. They have stumbled over the stumbling stone, as it is written, "Behold, I am laying in Zion a stone of stumbling, and a rock of offense; and whoever believes in him will not be put to shame." Brothers, my heart's desire and prayer to God for them is that they may be saved. For I bear them witness that they have a zeal for God, but not according to knowledge. For, being ignorant of the righteousness of God, and seeking to establish their own, they did not submit to God's righteousness. For Christ is the end of the law for righteousness to everyone who believes.

While Paul writes that these Israelites "...have a zeal for God...," the One, true God, he still desires and prays for them "...that they may be saved." Why? Because they were adding their good works to their faith, as if their good works were essential to save them. Paul writes that "...they did not pursue it by faith, but as if it were based on works." This ironically kept them from receiving salvation (righteousness), which is received by faith alone. They were trying to enter into a personal relationship with God based on their own righteousness. They rejected Jesus as the Messiah, who died in their place for their sins.

A works-righteousness system of getting right with God means that no one can really know if he or she has done enough good works to go to Heaven. You try your best and hope you go to the right place when you die. But God does not want us to live like that, with such great fear and uncertainty. The New Testament teaches that we can know, with certainty, that we are saved or have a relationship with God and are going to Heaven. This is true because God has taken action and done something that we can believe or trust in: Christ's death on the cross and His bodily resurrection. This was something that was done by God for us—not something that we do for God.

In John 5:24 Jesus says, "Truly, truly, I say to you, whoever hears my word and believes him who sent me has eternal life. He does not come into judgment, but has passed from death to life."

1 John 5:12–14 says, "Whoever has the Son has life; whoever does not have the Son of God does not have life. I write these things to you who believe in the name of the Son of God that you may know that you have eternal life."

The Bible also teaches us that once we have entered into a relationship with God, it is not kept up by our efforts or good works but is sustained by God. This too is a part of God's grace.

Romans 4:24–5:2 says, "It [righteousness] will be counted to us who believe in him who raised from the dead Jesus our Lord, who was delivered up for our trespasses and raised for our justification. Therefore, since we have been justified by faith, we have peace with God through our Lord Jesus Christ. Through him we have also obtained access by faith into this grace in which we stand, and we rejoice in hope of the glory of God."

At this point, one may ask, "What about all of the rules and commandments in the Bible? Do we ignore them because we're saved by grace?"

No. For God's Law and His commandments do have a place in our lives, but not to be the means where we try to earn salvation. Rather, they show us that we are sinners and in need of a Savior.

Romans 3:20 says, "...through the law comes knowledge of sin."

Galatians 3:24 says, "...the law was our guardian until Christ came, in order that we might be justified by faith."

Another great aspect of God's grace is that it helps us to keep our focus on the Lord, for trying to earn salvation through good works inevitably boomerangs back to put the focus of your relationship with God back onto yourself. You ask yourself, "Am I going to Heaven? Am I doing enough good to outweigh my bad? Do I really know God?"

In contrast, faith in Christ is vertical. It keeps the focus on God because He did all that was needed to bridge the gap between Himself and us.

Hebrews 12:1–2 says, "Therefore, since we are surrounded by so great a cloud of witnesses, let us also lay aside every weight, and sin which clings so closely, and let us run with endurance the race that is set before us, looking to Jesus, the founder and perfecter of our faith, who for the joy that was set before him endured the cross, despising the shame, and is seated at the right hand of the throne of God."

3

WHAT IS THE GOSPEL AND WHAT DOES IT MEAN TO BELIEVE IN THE GOSPEL?

In 1 Corinthians 15:3–8, Paul writes,
> For I delivered to you as of first importance what I also received: that Christ died for our sins in accordance with the Scriptures, that he was buried, that he was raised on the third day in accordance with the Scriptures, and that he appeared to Cephas [Peter], then to the twelve. Then he appeared to more than five hundred brothers at one time, most of whom are still alive, though some have fallen asleep. Then he appeared to James, then to all the apostles. Last of all, as to one untimely born, he appeared also to me.

In broader terms, the gospel's message is that all people are sinners, and our sin separates us from a loving God, our Creator, who wants to have a relationship with everyone. This can't occur through our good works, but only through faith in the death of Jesus Christ on the cross for our sins and His bodily resurrection from the dead. His death and resurrection pay the full price for all of our sins before God. When we believe this, God forgives us of all of our sins, gives us eternal life and a personal relationship with Him, and promises us that we will go to Heaven when we die.

When we repent of our sins and believe in the gospel, several other things happen:

*We are made into new creations by God. God transforms who we are. It's not a loss of personality or identity, but the loss of a wrong way of being and thinking. We are sinners and God's enemies by nature; therefore, we need new natures. We need new hearts and new minds.

2 Corinthians 5:17 says, "Therefore, if anyone is in Christ, he is a new creation. The old has passed away; behold, the new has come."

Galatians 6:15 says, "...neither circumcision counts for anything, nor uncircumcision, but a new creation."

*We receive eternal life.

In John 10:28, Jesus says, "I give them eternal life, and they will never perish, and no one will snatch them out of my hand." In John 17:3, He says, "And this is eternal life, that they know you the only true God, and Jesus Christ whom you have sent."

1 John 5:11–13 reads, "And this is the testimony, that God gave us eternal life, and this life is in his Son. Whoever has the Son has life; whoever does not have the Son of God does not have life. I write these things to you who believe in the name of the Son of God that you may know that you have eternal life."

*We have crossed over from death to life.

Jesus says in John 5:24, "Truly, truly, I say to you, whoever hears my word and believes him who sent me has eternal life. He does not come into judgment, but has passed from death to life."

*We receive Christ's righteousness. The Bible teaches that we receive the righteousness of Christ apart from any we may have on our own.

1 Corinthians 1:30 says, "...you are in Christ Jesus, who became to us wisdom from God, righteousness and sanctification and redemption."

2 Corinthians 5:21 says, "For our sake he made him to be sin who knew no sin, so that in him we might become the righteousness of God."

Philippians 3:8–9 reads, "Indeed, I count everything as loss because of the surpassing worth of knowing Christ Jesus my Lord. For his sake I have suffered the loss of all things and count them as rubbish, in order that I may gain Christ and be found in him, not having a righteousness of my own that comes from the law, but that which comes through faith in Christ, the righteousness from God that depends on faith."

Millard J. Erickson writes, "For what God does is actually to constitute us righteous by imputing (not imparting) the righteousness of Christ to us...For the penalty of sin has been paid, and thus the requirements of the law have been fulfilled. It is not a fiction, then, that believers are righteous, for the righteousness of Christ has been credited to them."[4]

---

[4] Millard J. Erickson, *Christian Theology,* 2nd ed. (Grand Rapids: Baker Books, 1998), 971.

When we believe in the gospel, our sin is removed from us. When God looks at a believer, it is like He is saying, "I know that you believe in the gospel. Therefore, when I see you, I don't see your sin, but the righteousness and perfection of Christ. When you die, then will you be made truly and actually righteous and perfect."

The Book of Hebrews describes Christ's death in the following ways: It saves believers completely (7:25), it gives believers eternal redemption (9:12), it makes believers holy (10:10), it makes us perfect forever (10:14), and where sins have been forgiven, there is no longer any sacrifice for sin (10:18).

The moment we die, we will no longer have sinful natures, but will be perfect. This means that we will neither sin nor even be tempted to sin in Heaven. This will be true freedom for all eternity.

4

WHY DID JESUS HAVE TO DIE?

After reading the first three chapters, one may ask, "That's all well and good, but why did Jesus have to die? Why did such a sacrifice have to be made? Since God is God, couldn't He have just forgiven all people? Or couldn't He forgive those who ask Him for forgiveness, but without the death of Christ?"

There are three main reasons why Jesus had to die, two of which we'll look at now. The first is that His death (and those of the animals that were sacrificed in the Old Testament) shows us the seriousness and severity of sin before God. While a lot can happen to a person in life, nothing is as striking and final as death. Death gets everyone's attention. God wanted for people to realize, even a little, just how serious sin is in His eyes.

The second reason why Jesus had to die is that He had to pay the price of our sins, which is death.

James 1:15b says that "sin when it is fully grown brings forth death."

Because of this, the Bible says that "the wages of sin is death" (Romans 6:23) and that "without the shedding of blood there is no forgiveness of sins" (Hebrews 9:22).

But what about the animal sacrifices of the Old Testament? Weren't they good enough?

Not really. Those were accepted by God, but they were only temporary. They were like a down payment. As the writer of Hebrews says, "For it is impossible for the blood of bulls and goats to take away sins" (Hebrews 10:4).

What about a person? Maybe someone else could pay for my sins?

This is better, and it gets closer, but it still doesn't work.

Psalm 49:7–9 says, "Truly no man can ransom another, or give to God the price of his life, for the ransom of their life is costly and can never suffice, that he should live on forever and never see the pit." This doesn't work because all people are sinners before God. Any other person, no matter how religious he or she may be, is still a sinner by nature and so is an inadequate sacrifice for another person.

So, we're all in the same boat. No one of us can pay the price for the sins of another, to say nothing of all humanity.

Jesus, as a true (but sinless) human being, is a perfect sacrifice for us. He's not an animal sacrifice, and He never sinned. Since Jesus doesn't have a sinful nature, He can truly and accurately take our place before the Father.

In Old Testament times, all sacrifices had to be perfect. As a sinless human being, Jesus was our perfect substitute. He was a true human being in all ways, but without sin.

1 John 3:5 says, "You know that he appeared in order to take away sins, and in him there is no sin."

How could Jesus not have a sinful nature and yet still be human? Through the virgin birth, when God created a special sinless human nature and body for Jesus. In this way, Jesus was sinless and truly human.

As Hebrews 10:5–7 says, "Consequently, when Christ came into the world, he said, 'Sacrifices and offerings you have not desired, but a body have you prepared for me; in burnt offerings and sin offerings you have taken no pleasure.' Then I said, 'Behold, I have come to do your will, O God, as it is written of me in the scroll of the book.'"

In fact, to be truly human is to not have a sinful nature. Remember back to Genesis when God created Adam and Eve as perfect (sinless) beings. Sin is something that we came up with, not God. Sin is just so natural to us that it appears to us as how things should be. However, God's original intent for all people was for us to be without sin.

Since we are sinners, our righteousness is like "a polluted garment" (Isaiah 64:6) in God's sight. In order to meet the standards of God's righteousness, only a perfect human being would be an adequate sacrifice for our sins. Christ lived a sinless, perfect life, and so He was the only acceptable substitute for us.

1 Peter 1:18–19 says, "...you were ransomed from the futile ways inherited from your forefathers, not with perishable things such as silver or gold, but with the precious blood of Christ, like that of a lamb without blemish or spot."

As Hebrews 7:25–27 says, "He is able to save to the uttermost those who draw near to God through him, since he always lives to make intercession for them. For it was indeed fitting that we should have such a high priest, holy, innocent, unstained, separated from sinners, and exalted above the heavens. He has no need, like those high priests, to offer sacrifices daily, first for his own sins and then for those of the people, since he did this once for all when he offered up himself."

The collective, or total, sin of all humankind was placed upon Jesus when He was on the cross. He paid the price for all peoples' sin. He died one death for all people of all eras, cultures, and countries. Therefore, all people can come into a relationship with God by trusting (believing) in Jesus' life, death, and bodily resurrection. The way to a relationship with God is the same for everyone.

1 Peter 3:18 says, "For Christ also suffered once for sins, the righteous for the unrighteous, that he might bring us to God."

This is one reason why Jesus had to be fully God. Along with being a sinless person, Jesus had to be God in order to be an acceptable sacrifice for our sins. For if Jesus was just a human being (even a sinless one), there would have still been something missing from Him being a full and complete sacrifice for our sins.

Remember that our sin violates God's eternal nature. As people, we do not have eternal natures; we have a literal beginning in time and space. But God in His nature has no beginning and no end. Since our sins are primarily against God, a being who is eternal, the punishment for our sins had to be eternal. Since God is eternal, only He could perfectly pay the penalty of our sins. It takes God to pay off a God-sized debt. So Jesus, our substitute, had to be fully God. He could die, or be separated from God, for us. A Jesus that is not God is not a sufficient sacrifice for our sins.

Erickson writes, "If the redemption accomplished on the cross is to avail for humankind, it must be the work of the human Jesus. But if it is to have the infinite value necessary to atone for the sins of all human beings in relationship to an infinite and perfectly holy God, then it must be the work of the divine Christ as well. If the death of the Savior is not the work of a unified God-man, it will be deficient at one point or the other."[5]

We know that the worse the crime committed, the greater the punishment. Take our country's laws, for example. Generally speaking, the greater the offense, the greater the punishment. Our offense, or sin against God, is the ultimate "crime." And what comes with that, accordingly, is the ultimate punishment.

But just as one person can pay off the financial debt of another, so Jesus paid off the debt of our sin to God. We can say to God that Jesus paid the price in full for our sins.

---

[5] Millard J. Erickson, *Christian Theology*, 2nd ed. (Grand Rapids: Baker Books, 1998), 740.

Another way to look at it is like this. A news story I saw recently talked about a "suspended pizza."

It's an Italian tradition that started sixty years ago. In the current difficult economic times, it is making a comeback in the home of the pizza: Naples, Italy.

The simple idea is this: a customer pays in advance for a pizza for someone else—a total stranger.

You may have heard of something similar here in America, where someone would buy a cup of coffee for the person behind him or her in the drive-through. But that chain only lasted for a very short amount of time—maybe for five or six customers. Then someone would break the chain and not pay for the next person, and that would be it.

This is different, in that it is ongoing, and the person getting the free pizza may not be the next in line, come in that hour, or even come in that day.

At the shop, the pizzeria owner keeps track of how many free pizzas have been paid for and marks it on a board outside. If someone needs a free pizza, that person comes in, asks for one, and it's already been paid for.

The news report showed that the owner's board said "forty-three pizzas." That's forty-three pizzas that were paid for by others so that those who couldn't afford them could also enjoy a meal out.[6]

It's an illustration of what Jesus Christ did when He died on the cross for our sins. Obviously, what He did was of infinitely greater worth, but the idea of substitution is the same. It's a sacrifice.

It's one person paying in full for something that another person could not afford to pay for on his or her own.

Christ died and was separated from God for us, so now we, as sinners, can say that while we could never pay off the debt by our own efforts, we could point to Someone who was a substitute for us. We can say to God that Jesus paid the price in full for our sins.

1 Peter 2:24 says, "He himself bore our sins in his body on the tree, that we might die to sin and live to righteousness. By his wounds you have been healed." And 1 Peter 3:18a says, "For Christ also suffered once for sins, the righteous for the unrighteous, that he might bring us to God."

---

[6] "Italy: Suspended Pizza," *European Journal* (July 31, 2013): http://dw.de/p/195SR

Romans 5:6–10:
> For while we were still weak, at the right time Christ died for the ungodly. For one will scarcely die for a righteous person—though perhaps for a good person one would dare even to die—but God shows his love for us in that while we were still sinners, Christ died for us. Since, therefore, we have now been justified by his blood, much more shall we be saved by him from the wrath of God. For if while we were enemies we were reconciled to God by the death of his Son, much more, now that we are reconciled, shall we be saved by his life.

2 Corinthians 5:21, in very striking language, says, "For our sake he made him to be sin who knew no sin, so that in him we might become the righteousness of God."

John the Baptist called Jesus "...the Lamb of God, who takes away the sin of the world!" (John 1:29).

In the next chapter, we'll start by looking at the third reason that Jesus had to die and another reason why Jesus had to be God.

5

WHY DID JESUS HAVE TO BE GOD?

Who was Jesus? Was He a mere human being? Was He only a great teacher? Was He one who was in touch with the Christ Consciousness? Or, was He the Archangel Michael?

Actually, He was none of the above. The Bible teaches that Jesus was fully human and fully God at the same time.

Some of the clearest Scriptures that state that Jesus Christ is God are the following:

John 1:1–3 states, "In the beginning was the Word, and the Word was with God, and the Word was God. He was in the beginning with God. All things were made through Him, and without Him was not any thing made that was made."

Colossians 1:16–19 says, "... by him all things were created, in heaven and on earth, visible and invisible, whether thrones or dominions or rulers or authorities—all things were created through him and for him. And he is before all things, and in him all things hold together. And he is the head of the body, the church. He is the beginning, the firstborn from the dead, that in everything he might be preeminent. For in him all the fullness of God was pleased to dwell."

Colossians 2:9 reads, "For in him the whole fullness of deity dwells bodily."

Not only did Jesus have to be a 100 percent human, He also had to be 100 percent totally and fully God. Why?

Let's take a look at the third reason why Jesus had to die. That reason is love, and we'll see how it weaves into why Jesus had to be God.

While God shows His love to humanity in many ways every day, Christ's death for our sins was the primary way that God showed us His love.

Romans 5:8 says, "But God shows his love for us in that while we were still sinners, Christ died for us."

The Bible says that God is love. Love is many things, and one of these things is action.

John 3:16–17 says, "For God so loved the world, that he gave his only Son, that whoever believes in him should not perish but have eternal life. For God did not send his Son into the world to condemn the world, but in order that the world might be saved through him."

Here we see that because God loved the world, He acted. God didn't sit back and say, "Oh, how I love the world. It is nice to love the world. I'll just sit here and love the world." No. Because God loved the world, His love led Him to action. Because God loved the world, He wanted to help people get out of their sinful states and into a relationship with Him.

To understand why this means that Jesus had to be God and die for our sins, let's think about ways that one person can show love to another.

At the basic level, love can be shown through words. One can say, "I love you." That is nice, and depending on the length of the relationship, maybe a bit risky, but there is no direct cost or sacrifice involved. Three words are spoken or penned (hopefully not texted if it's for the first time!), and that is all.

We know that merely saying words without any action doesn't mean very much. When actions follow the words, then we see true love. And the greater the love, the greater we are willing to pay or sacrifice to show our love. Now we enter into the level of sacrifice as a way to show our love for another.

The first way of acting out our love may be to buy a present for our beloved. This is doing more than just saying, "I love you." While it's not a huge sacrifice, it is a start.

After this, you might help someone without thought or expectation of repayment—a sacrifice of your time.

We can go gradually up the ladder of sacrifice until we come to your most valuable possession: your life. Surely, as we can understand love, there is no greater sacrifice than to give your life for another. We can give of our time, money, and material possessions, all of these to various degrees, but the ultimate show of our love is to give our lives.

Jesus says, "Greater love has no one than this, that someone lay down his life for his friends" (John 15:13).

This is why God Himself had to die for humanity. There could be no greater demonstration, no greater example of God's love, than for Him to truly become one of us and die on our behalf.

You may ask the question, "How can God die?" Of course, God can't die, but Jesus, who was fully human, can. One way to look at the separation between the man Jesus and God the Father is in the following analogy:

Two people can be sitting at a table together and yet feel miles apart. Perhaps you've experienced this yourself.

The two may be physically close, but because of some problem or disagreement, they can literally feel far apart. In the same way, while Jesus was always God, at the time He took the penalty of all of our sins onto Himself, He could feel God the Father turning His back on Him. This was the agony that Christ faced on the cross, which was even greater than the tremendous physical pain He endured.

While there is a mystery to God becoming a man and dying, there is no mystery as to what this sacrifice says about His love for us. All people around the world can understand and appreciate the ultimate sacrifice of one person giving his or her life for another.

The gospel is universal, and the basis of the gospel, God's love for humanity, can be understood and appreciated by anyone anytime. This is something that any group of people from anywhere in the world can relate to. It can be comprehended by any culture, in any language, and at any time in human history.

The collective (total) sin of all humankind was placed upon Jesus when He was on the cross. He paid the price for all peoples' sin. He died one death for all people of all times, cultures, and countries. All people have sinned, and our sin separates us from God. Therefore, by His one death for all people's sins, all people can come into a relationship with God by trusting (believing) in Jesus' life, death, and resurrection—by believing that Jesus' death was the one, only, full, and final payment for our sins. The way to have a personal relationship with God is the same for everyone.

You couldn't invent a god or a story of a god suffering or more aligning itself with humanity than is exemplified in the God of the Bible. Jesus suffered as a human being though the temptations, trials, disappointments, and hurts of life. And He suffered most while on the cross, with His anguish at its worst.

The Bible says that God is love. True love always forgives. If you are to have a true, godly relationship with someone, whether as husband and wife or with a good friend, there must be forgiveness. This is a key to the success of any good relationship. True forgiveness is not someone saying, "Oh, okay, I'll forgive you," or, "I'll forgive you this time, but I don't know about the next." It's not like that at all. Forgiveness is both an attitude and a desire. Not only does love forgive, but love wants to forgive. Love looks for ways to forgive. When one person has sinned against another, and the person in the wrong asks for forgiveness, the love of the offended party immediately grants forgiveness and does so willingly and with joy.

This is why God sent His Son Jesus to die for us on the cross. God wants to forgive us because He loves us.

Something else to consider when thinking about Jesus' death on the cross is that He wasn't forced to die for our sins. He wasn't tricked into doing it. But He died for us from His own free will. From His love for His creation, humanity, He agreed to go to the cross on our behalf.

Jesus said, "'Now is my soul troubled. And what shall I say? "Father, save me from this hour?" But for this purpose I have come to this hour. Father, glorify your name.' Then a voice came from heaven: 'I have glorified it, and I will glorify it again'" (John 12:27–28).

That's true sacrifice. That's true giving. If I'm forced to do something and I comply, that's nothing to admire. That's not praiseworthy. But Jesus freely gave of Himself. He was obedient to everything the Father asked of Him, including being tortured, dying on the cross, and being separated from the Father. He did all of this for our benefit.

As Romans 5:7–8 says, "For one will scarcely die for a righteous person—though perhaps for a good person one would dare even to die—but God shows his love for us in that while we were still sinners, Christ died for us."

Jesus said, "But for this purpose I have come to this hour" (John 12:27).

There were no other options. There was no "plan B."

This was the only plan. There was a task to be completed, and it had to be fulfilled.

In the Garden of Gethsemane, when the temptation to avoid the cross perhaps hit its peak, even then Jesus said, "Yet not what I will, but what you will" (Mark 14:36).

Take a moment to reflect on select verses from the hymn "When I Survey the Wondrous Cross" by Isaac Watts.

When I survey the wondrous cross
On which the Prince of glory died,
My richest gain I count but loss,
And pour contempt on all my pride.

Forbid it, Lord, that I should boast,
Save in the death of Christ my God!
All the vain things that charm me most,
I sacrifice them to His blood.

See from His head, His hands, His feet,
Sorrow and love flow mingled down!
Did e'er such love and sorrow meet,
Or thorns compose so rich a crown? [7]

---

[7] http://www.cyberhymnal.org/htm/w/h/e/whenisur.htm

6

WHY DID JESUS HAVE TO RISE FROM THE DEAD?

Jesus' resurrection showed that He was truly sent from God, because only God has the power over sin and death. It also shows us that Jesus was God, because the Bible says that Jesus rose Himself from the dead.

In John 2:19-21, Jesus said, ""Destroy this temple, and in three days I will raise it up." The Jews then said, "It has taken forty-six years to build this temple, and will you raise it up in three days?" But he was speaking about the temple of his body."

All of the other world's religious leaders throughout history died and stayed dead. Only Jesus rose again.

Christ died and then truly came to life again in the same body in which He died, but glorified. He ate with His disciples and had Thomas, who had doubted His resurrection, feel His wounds.

Jesus said to His disciples, "'See my hands and my feet, that it is I myself. Touch me, and see. For a spirit does not have flesh and bones as you see that I have.' And when he had said this, he showed them his hands and his feet. And while they still disbelieved for joy and were marveling, he said to them, 'Have you anything here to eat?' They gave him a piece of broiled fish, and he took it and ate before them" (Luke 24:39–42).

"Then he said to Thomas, 'Put your finger here, and see my hands; and put out your hand, and place it in my side. Do not disbelieve, but believe.' Thomas answered him, 'My Lord and my God!' (John 20:27–28).

Jesus' resurrection was a victory over sin and death. It's a victory that Jesus gives to all who believe in Him.

To people who were skeptical of the resurrection, Paul writes in 1 Corinthians 15:54-57, "Death is swallowed up in victory." "O death, where is your victory? O death, where is your sting?" The sting of death is sin, and the power of sin is the law. But thanks be to God, who gives us the victory through our Lord Jesus Christ."

God invites all people to share in this victory over death. No one needs to be afraid of where they will go when they die, because Jesus has bridged the gap that our sin has created between us and the Lord. We simply acknowledge that fact and, by faith, we enter into a personal relationship with the living God.

Jesus predicted His resurrection, which also shows that He was a true prophet.

"See, we are going up to Jerusalem, and the Son of Man will be delivered over to the chief priests and the scribes, and they will condemn him to death and deliver him over to the Gentiles. And they will mock him and spit on him, and flog him and kill him. And after three days he will rise" (Mark 10:33–34).

Jesus' death and resurrection assures us that we no longer have to live under the power of Satan. Through the resurrection of Jesus Christ, God gives those who believe the gospel the power to both live for the Lord and to be changed people.

We can live changed lives!

We can be different from our old selves!

Paul writes that all believers can know, "...what is the immeasurable greatness of his power toward us who believe, according to the working of his great might that he worked in Christ when he raised him from the dead and seated him at his right hand in the heavenly places" (Ephesians 1:19-20).

Through the gospel of Jesus Christ, God not only forgives us of our sins and promises us an eternity with Him, but He also cares about our lives and who we are in the here and now. Jesus is our Savior. He doesn't just save us from the penalty of our sins; He saves us from the power of sin as well. That's true freedom, friends. And it can only be found in the Lord Jesus Christ.

In John 8:34-36, Jesus says, "Truly, truly, I say to you, everyone who practices sin is a slave to sin. The slave does not remain in the house forever; the son remains forever. So if the Son sets you free, you will be free indeed."

Galatians 5:1 says, "For freedom Christ has set us free; stand firm therefore, and do not submit again to a yoke of slavery."

This freedom from sin is something that all people long for, whether they recognize it as such or not. It only comes through the power of the Holy Spirit in your life. You receive the Holy Spirit by professing faith in the gospel and all that it means; the deity, sinless life, death on the cross and bodily resurrection of Jesus Christ as full payment for all of our sins.

The death and resurrection of Jesus Christ takes care of all of humanity's basic needs. That includes the need to enter into a personal relationship with God, the need to go to Heaven when we die, and also the need to live godly lives, having power over the sin and temptations in our lives.

Christ's resurrection completes His sacrifice for our sins. Christianity stands or falls on the bodily resurrection of Jesus Christ.

This is a clear point of separation between Christianity and all of the world's other religions. Only Jesus has defeated sin and death. Only Jesus became alive after He died.

In Acts 2:24, Peter says, "God raised him up, loosing the pangs of death, because it was not possible for him to be held by it."

Constantly throughout the Book of Acts, we see the disciples preaching Jesus' resurrection from the dead. Over and over again, we see this. The early Church knew that this was the main thing.

Now take a moment to reflect on select verses from the hymn, "Because He Lives."

God sent His Son
They called Him Jesus
He came to love, heal and forgive
He lived and died to buy my pardon
An empty grave is there to prove my Savior lives

Because He lives I can face tomorrow
Because He lives all fear is gone
Because I know He holds the future
And life is worth the living just because He lives

How sweet to hold a newborn baby,
And feel the pride and joy he gives.
But greater still the calm assurance,
This child can face uncertain days because He lives.

Because He lives I can face tomorrow
Because He lives all fear is gone
Because I know He holds the future
And life is worth the living just because He lives[8]

---

[8] http://jesusreigns.wordpress.com/2008/10/15/because-he-lives-lyrics

7

WHY IS FAITH IN JESUS THE ONLY WAY TO KNOW GOD?

The Bible teaches that there are not many ways to enter into a personal relationship with God.

Jesus, in the Garden of Gethsemane, prayed, "My Father, if this cannot pass unless I drink it, your will be done" (Matthew 26:42).

Since Jesus did in fact die on the cross and was resurrected by the Father from the dead, this means that faith in Jesus' death and resurrection was how God chose for people to be saved. There was no other way for God to have people come into a relationship with Him (as we saw in chapter four). If there was another way, then Christ would not have needed to die.

Acts 4:12 says, "And there is salvation in no one else, for there is no other name under heaven given among men by which we must be saved."

In John 14:6, Jesus says, "I am the way, and the truth, and the life. No one comes to the Father except through me."

Hebrews 10:17–18 says, "I will remember their sins and their lawless deeds no more." Where there is forgiveness of these, there is no longer any offering for sin."

Galatians 2:21 says, "If righteousness were through the law, then Christ died for no purpose."

Society in general likes to believe that there can be many ways to know God, that many of the world religions can bring a devoted follower into a relationship with God and provide a way to Heaven. Yet this is not true, because only Christianity adequately deals with the penalty of our sin and our sinful natures through the death and bodily resurrection of one Person: Jesus Christ. All other major world religions teach that it's ultimately by one's good works that someone can go to Heaven. Yet, we've seen that this is not true. No one can ever do enough good works to pay for his or her sins or tilt the scale in favor of "good works" over "sins."

Another reason for saying that faith in Jesus is the only way to God and Heaven is that Scripture teaches us that there is only one true God in existence.

Isaiah 43:10b–11 says, "Before me no god was formed, nor shall there be any after me. I, I am the Lord, and besides me there is no savior."

Psalms 86:8, and 86:10 say, "There is none like you among the gods, O Lord, nor are there any works like yours...you are great and do wondrous things; you alone are God."

Now one may say, "Okay, but what of the illustration of one God being at the top of the mountain and each of the world's religions acting as a road that eventually leads to this one God?" Or you may say, "Yes, there is only one true God, but this one true God is known by several different names—Jesus, Allah, Jehovah, etc."

I admit that this illustration and statement that followed it are interesting ways of holding to monotheism on one hand, while saying that there are many true religions on the other. But on close inspection, it doesn't work. When you go a little deeper, it is clear that religions differ on the most fundamental and important points—who God is, and how to get to Heaven.

For example, this God at the top of the mountain must be the same in His nature for all religions. Christians believe that Jesus Christ is fully God. Yet, Jehovah's Witnesses, Jews, and Muslims (among others) reject this belief. Since we are dealing with the very nature of God, then it must be true that not all of these religions believe in the same God. Jesus cannot both be God by nature and not be God at the same time.

The Latter-Day Saints (Mormons), Hindus, and some Eastern religions teach that God in nature is one with the universe.[9] In contrast, Christianity teaches that God is not one with the universe, but is separate from His creation. That's quite a fundamental difference concerning the nature of God. Therefore, it is impossible for these different religions to all be leading to the same God.

What do we say about atheists or Satanists? Are they going to Heaven too? Atheists don't believe in God or Heaven. Are they going down the same road as someone with devout religious beliefs? Satanists follow the devil and work against God. Can a Satanist and a Christian really be following the same God?

Some may argue that this teaching is too exclusive. In response, let's remember that sometimes the truth can be very exclusive.

---

[9] http://www.lds.org/topics/creation?lang=eng
http://www.lds.org/ensign/1998/01/in-the-beginning-a-latter-day-perspective?lang=eng

Two plus two always equals four. It never equals five, two, or twenty, but always equals four. Now, that's pretty exclusive. But it is also true.

This truth is not really exclusive when looked at objectively and when we see the big picture. For while there is only one way to know one God, this one God wants everyone to enter into a personal relationship with Him. God wants all people to receive salvation and forgiveness of their sins. God is an inclusive God, and the gospel is universal. This is something that can get missed when we speak of there being only one God and of Jesus being the only way to know God and go to Heaven. God wants everyone to be saved. The free offer of salvation goes out to all people around the world—Muslims, Hindus, literate, illiterate, rich, poor, you name it. God wants everybody to enter into His Kingdom.

To illustrate this truth, Jesus told a parable from which I'd like to quote:

> A man once gave a great banquet and invited many. And at the time for the banquet he sent his servant to say to those who had been invited, "Come, for everything is now ready."...Then the master of the house...said to his servant, "Go out quickly to the streets and lanes of the city, and bring in the poor and crippled and blind and lame."
>
> And the servant said, "Sir, what you commanded has been done, and still there is room." And the master said to the servant, "Go out to the highways and hedges and compel people to come in, that my house may be filled" (Luke 14:16–17, 14:21–23).

Ezekiel 18:23 says, "Have I any pleasure in the death of the wicked, declares the Lord God, and not rather that he should turn from his way and live?" Ezekiel 18:32 adds, "For I have no pleasure in the death of anyone, declares the Lord God; so turn, and live."

1 Timothy 2:3–6 says, "God our Savior, who desires all people to be saved and to come to the knowledge of the truth. For there is one God, and there is one mediator between God and men, the man Christ Jesus, who gave himself as a ransom for all, which is the testimony given at the proper time."

2 Peter 3:9 says, "The Lord is not slow to fulfill his promise as some count slowness, but is patient toward you, not wishing that any should perish, but that all should reach repentance."

But this free gift of salvation must be received.

Revelation 22:17 says, "The Spirit and the Bride say, 'Come.' And let the one who hears say, 'Come.' And let the one who is thirsty come; let the one who desires take the water of life without price."

It is important to clarify here that I don't believe that my church or denomination is the only way to God. But the Bible teaches that Jesus Christ Himself is the only way to God.

In John 3:36, Jesus says, "Whoever believes in the Son has eternal life; whoever does not obey the Son shall not see life, but the wrath of God remains on him."

While the only way to receive eternal life is by believing in the Son, the offer is inclusive. "That whoever believes" literally means *anyone*.

8

WHY DO PEOPLE GO TO HELL?

God didn't create people with the intention that any would go to Hell. But God gave them free will, with which they can choose to be with Him or reject Him.

> Luke 16:19–23 says,
> There was a rich man who was clothed in purple and fine linen and who feasted sumptuously every day. And at his gate was laid a poor man named Lazarus, covered with sores, who desired to be fed with what fell from the rich man's table. Moreover, even the dogs came and licked his sores. The poor man died and was carried by the angels to Abraham's side. The rich man also died and was buried, and in Hades, being in torment, he lifted up his eyes and saw Abraham far off and Lazarus at his side.

Jude 1:7 reads, "Sodom and Gomorrah and the surrounding cities, which likewise indulged in sexual immorality and pursued unnatural desire, serve as an example by undergoing a punishment of eternal fire."

Revelation 20:14–15 says, "Then Death and Hades were thrown into the lake of fire. This is the second death, the lake of fire. And if anyone's name was not found written in the book of life, he was thrown into the lake of fire."

Surely there must be another place for people to exist after they die than to be with God. And there is: Hell. Hell is a place where God does not reside in the fullness of His presence and blessings.

Some may not like this, and that is perfectly understandable. As we've seen earlier, God doesn't want people to go to Hell. No one should want anyone to go to Hell. Yet at the same time, there has to be a place for people who don't want to live forever with God.

One could say that instead of Hell, Universalism has an answer—the belief that everyone goes to Heaven. This concept may sound good initially, but it has some problems. Most importantly, it contradicts the clear teachings of the Bible.

Secondly, what of those who don't want to go to Heaven? Why should all people be forced to live forever with a God they either hate or in which they don't believe? Why should they be forced to spend eternity in a place where they don't want to be?

If everyone goes to Heaven, does this include atheists? Atheists don't believe in God or Heaven, so how can they end up in Heaven after they die? Do Satan worshipers also go to Heaven? Why should they be allowed in Heaven?

Third, in a Universalistic worldview, why should God allow someone into Heaven? On what grounds should that person be allowed? What about that person's sin and sinful natures?

What about God's justice? According to Universalists, everyone will eventually make it into Heaven. The terrorists responsible for the events of September 11, 2001, Hitler, Stalin, everyone gets in. But what about justice for those who were wronged?

Sometimes this charge is leveled against Christianity when someone makes a deathbed statement of faith. It is said that it's not fair if one can live a life rank with sin, then enter into Heaven just by believing in Jesus right before his or her death.

But there is a great difference between a Universalist's view and that of a Christian.

With Christianity, justice has been served by Christ's death on the cross and bodily resurrection from death. Christ paid the price for all of our sins, including the person who has a deathbed conversion.

But with Universalism, there is no justice. Hitler can kill millions, die, and go to Heaven. This makes God unjust and unfair. And we know that He's neither of these things.

Some posit reincarnation as an answer, but the Bible says that people have this one life to decide to believe in God or reject Him.

Hebrews 9:27–28 reads, "And just as it is appointed for man to die once, and after that comes judgment, so Christ, having been offered once to bear the sins of many, will appear a second time, not to deal with sin but to save those who are eagerly waiting for him."

Some say that God sends people to Hell and so it's God's fault that anyone goes there. But God does not send anyone to Hell. God sends people to Hell the same way an airline ticket agent sends someone onto an airplane.

People decide to go where they want, make all the arrangements, get their luggage and documents together, go to the airport, and check in all on their own. When a person asks the ticket agent for his or her boarding pass and receives it, the agent is not forcing the passenger to get on the plane. This was a choice that the passenger made on his or her own. The ticket agent confirms the passenger's choice that he or she made earlier.

Those who enter into a relationship with God before they die will be with God in Heaven forever after death. Those who do not want to have a relationship with God will not be forced by Him to do so. They will go to Hell by their own choice. So by their own free wills, they will choose to be apart from God, and this decision will be made permanent upon death, with no second chances.

Some say that because of Hell, God isn't really loving. That if God was truly love, then He wouldn't send anyone to Hell. When people reject Him, they should be able to live in a place much like Earth is now, with joy, love, peace, and happiness. It wouldn't be a place like Hell—with nonstop pain, suffering, and torment. The argument says that God is really being childish in sending people to Hell for not accepting Him. It makes God out to be a spoiled brat throwing a temper tantrum.

But let's take a look at this from the flip side, from the perspective of the person who rejects God.

This point of view wants all of God's blessings, but nothing of God Himself. This person hates God, but loves God's blessings (peace, love, joy, enjoyment of material possessions). What kind of attitude is that? It is self-centered.

If you say "no" to God, then you say "no" to all of God—to all of His love, joy, and peace. Why is this so?

The only reason we have love, joy, and peace on this earth and in our lives is because of God. They come from God Himself. They originate in Him. We can't have these things apart from Him.

1 John 4:8b says, "God is love."

James 1:17 says, "Every good gift and every perfect gift is from above, coming down from the Father of lights."

If you say that you don't want anything to do with God Himself, on a personal, relational level, then you are also saying no to His love, joy, and peace. It's a package deal. They all come from God.

Therefore, without God, there can be only Hell. There can be only suffering and torment.

There is a bit of irony here, in that people who hold to the aforementioned view do have it partially correct. Temporarily correct, in that people here and now can enjoy God's blessings and benefits and say that He doesn't exist.

They can write books saying He doesn't exist. They can go on talk shows and debates saying He doesn't exist. All the while, they are enjoying His blessings—life, health, peace, joy, the beauty of nature, etc. God blesses those who reject Him.

As Jesus says in Matthew 5:45, "…he makes his sun rise on the evil and on the good, and sends rain on the just and on the unjust."

When witnessing to unbelievers at Lystra, Paul said, "he did not leave himself without witness, for he did good by giving you rains from heaven and fruitful seasons, satisfying your hearts with food and gladness" (Acts 14:17).

Proverbs 29:13 says, "The poor man and the oppressor meet together; the Lord gives light to the eyes of both."

In Job 22:17–18a, it says, "They said to God, 'Depart from us,' and 'What can the Almighty do to us?' Yet he filled their houses with good things."

So how does this work? It's because this is a special time. It's a unique time in which we can look at both God and Satan, God and evil, and decide which side we want to be on for all eternity. Whom do we want to live with, and whom do we want to live for?

For now, you can enjoy God's blessings and still reject Him. But God gives people blessings not so that they will reject Him, but so that they will "taste and see that the Lord is good!" (Psalm 34:8) and believe in Him and come to "love the Lord your God with all your heart and with all your soul and with all your mind and with all your strength" (Mark 12:30).

As we've seen, whatever decision we make by the time we die, that decision will be permanent.

Some may say that God should give second chances for people to believe in Him after they die. It's an interesting argument. After all, God's nature doesn't change when someone dies; His love and desire for the person to enter into a personal relationship with Him will always stay the same. While there is not a specific Bible chapter and verse that I can give to answer why God does not offer people opportunities to believe in Him after they die, we can still take a look at the subject.

As we've just seen, it is clear that the Bible does say that there are no second chances to believe after death.

Why is this so? One thought is that while God is always a God of grace and love, people can choose to reject Him, and those who do so on earth will always choose to reject Him after they die. Even in Hell, no one will turn in true faith to the Lord. Their hearts, which were hardened while on earth, will become so hardened that true repentance and belief will be impossible. The person's heart will be so hardened that no One and nothing will change the person's mind.

As William Lane Craig said in his debate with Craig Bradley, "It is possible that persons in hell grow only more implacable in their hatred of God as time goes on. Rather than repent and ask God for forgiveness, they continue to curse Him and reject Him. God thus has no choice but to leave them where they are."[10]

C. S. Lewis says in the book *The Problem of Pain* that "the door to Hell is locked from the inside."[11]

In the same debate, William Lane Craig gives us another point to consider:

> If a person commits an infinite number of sins, then the sum total of all such sins deserves infinite punishment. Now, of course, nobody commits an infinite number of sins in the earthly life. But what about in the afterlife? Insofar as the inhabitants of hell continue to hate God and reject Him, they continue to sin and so accrue to themselves more guilt and more punishment. In a real sense, then, hell is self-perpetuating. In such a case, every sin has a finite punishment, but because sinning goes on forever, so does the punishment.[12]

As stated earlier, while there is no specific verse to look up, we can conclude that people in Hell are there because they don't want anything to do with God—literally forever.

---

[10] William Lane Craig and Ray Bradley, "Can a Loving God Send People to Hell?" *Reasonable Faith* (1994): http://www.reasonablefaith.org/can-a-loving-god-send-people-to-hell-the-craig-bradley-debate

[11] C. S. Lewis, *The Problem of Pain* (New York: Macmillan, 1944), 130.

[12] Craig and Bradley, "Can a Loving God."

Even if God were to offer salvation to such people once a day for a thousand years, the answer from them would be "no" every time.

Something else to consider is that the basis that we come to know God is by faith. At the great white throne of judgment, all people will see God (Philippians 2:12) and at that time, there will no longer be an opportunity for faith. God will be right there; the time for faith will have passed.

The choice is ours to repent of our sins and believe in the gospel—the deity of Jesus Christ, in His death on the cross that paid the price in full for all of our sins, and in His bodily resurrection from the dead—or to say "no" to God and refuse to believe in Him.

Of course, God and us, His followers, want for everyone to experience the fullness of God. God doesn't want for anyone to go to Hell, but rather to have a personal relationship with Him. He wants us to experience all of His love, joy, and peace—and there's even more to God than that.

9

HOW CAN I PERSONALLY KNOW GOD?

Even if you don't feel like a rebel or one of God's enemies, you may feel that something is missing in your life. You know that there must be more to the life you are living. Or you feel guilt over the wrongs you have done, and nothing you've tried will make that guilt go away.

Perhaps you look at the beautiful world all around you and the stars above, and you think that there must be a Creator. And you think that maybe He can be known. Maybe there is something to all you've heard about Heaven and life after death.

God wants a relationship with you to be based on love. Love, by definition, can't be forced. Since God is the Creator of all humanity, He wants everyone (His creations) to be with Him. God created people to have perfect relationships with Him.

In contrast, love does not consist of cold rules and regulations. Nor is it a matter of just doing the best you can and hoping you make it to Heaven.

Love is God saying to you, "Come on in and let's share a meal together." But in order to do that, you need for there to be a way to choose to enter into a relationship with God. For the relationship to be truly loving, it must be a choice. It must be entered into freely. Even with the Holy Spirit opening people's hearts to the truth and reality of the gospel, at some point they must say with their hearts and minds, "Yes! This is true. I believe it. I want to enter into a personal relationship with God. I want Him to forgive me of all of my sins and take me to Heaven when I die."

We can come to God anytime by doing two things: repenting of our sins and believing in the gospel.

Repentance means acknowledging our sinfulness before God. We must admit that we have broken His laws, not believed in Him, and understand that our sins separate us from God. Believing the gospel means trusting in Jesus Christ—His deity, death on the cross, and resurrection from the dead as full payment for our sins.

Please note that you can come to Christ with questions and doubts about Him, the Bible, and the church. You can come to Him with your sins, problems, and troubles. That's okay.

That's the only way we can come to God, openly and honestly. Come to Him just as you are right now. God wants to have an open, honest, and loving relationship with you. He has paid the price for all of your sins, past, present, and future. Not one of your sins has gone unpaid for, and not one is so great that He can't forgive you. He can replace your feeling of guilt with the assurance of a right standing before Him. There is absolutely nothing to fear by coming to the Lord, for God is love and He beckons you to believe in Him and have a personal relationship with Him.

APPENDIX

A

DO I HAVE TO BE BAPTIZED IN ORDER TO GO TO HEAVEN?

Some say that in order to enter into a personal relationship with God and go to Heaven, you must be baptized. This is not true. Baptism is important and has its place, but not as a way for someone to receive salvation.

Those who teach baptismal regeneration are using baptism as a way to receive salvation by good works. Consider what goes into being baptized. When you are to be baptized, you may first be required to attend some sort of class, then arrangements are made for the location, date, and time of the rite, you need to travel there, and then go through the act of baptism (which includes doing certain things and speaking certain words). Besides that, at least one other person has to be there to say certain words and perform the ceremony. If this is all solely the work of God, as some argue, then why does it require you and the one performing the baptism to physically go somewhere and do all of these things?

When one says that you have to do more than repent and believe in order to be saved, that is adding works to the gospel of grace. We've seen that Scripture teaches that people are saved and enter into a personal relationship with God by faith alone. If you trust in something or someone besides the gospel (i.e., baptism) for your salvation, then you believe that your good works will be good enough to save you. This will not be enough, however, for you cannot be saved by your good works, even if you are following the one true God. We saw this in chapter one when we looked at Romans 9:30–10:5.

Another way to view this is to look at the Atonement. Since Christ paid the full price for our sins, then why do we need to be baptized in order to be saved? Isn't Christ's death on the cross sufficient? Of course it is. It is wrong to make an act of obedience to Christ (which is what baptism is) into a qualification for salvation (which it is not).

Let's look at some Scriptures that show you do not need to be baptized in order to enter into a personal relationship with the Lord.

Acts 10:44–48:
> While Peter was still saying these things, the Holy Spirit fell on all who heard the word.
>
> 45 And the believers from among the circumcised who had come with Peter were amazed, because the gift of the Holy Spirit was poured out even on the Gentiles. 46 For they were hearing them speaking in tongues and extolling God. Then Peter declared, 47 "Can anyone withhold water for baptizing these people, who have received the Holy Spirit just as we have?" 48 And he commanded them to be baptized in the name of Jesus Christ. Then they asked him to remain for some days.

Here we see that people are saved before they are baptized. That Cornelius and his household received salvation is shown by their receiving the Holy Spirit (v. 45). Their salvation was demonstrated to Peter and the brothers by Cornelius and the others speaking in tongues (v.46). It is only after this that Peter says they should be baptized with water (v. 47). If there is any doubt about Cornelius and his household being true believers, notice what Peter says before they are baptized, "They have received the Holy Spirit just as we have" (v. 47).

Some may say that Cornelius and his household are just an anomaly, that this is simply an exception to the rule. But there is nothing in Scripture to lead us to believe that this is true.

First, the Bible does not treat this episode like an anomaly but as a straightforward occurrence. Second, Luke doesn't mention a lack of water for baptism. When it came time for them to be baptized, they were baptized without any problems. Third, no one was sick or dying, and so couldn't be baptized. There is nothing special or out of the ordinary happening here. Cornelius and his family believed, were saved, and then were baptized.

Just before this text, Peter says, "All the prophets testify about him that everyone who believes in him receives forgiveness of sins through his name" (Acts 10:43). Again, we see forgiveness through belief alone without any mention of baptism.

Similarly, in Acts 9:17–18, Saul (later to be known as Paul) is filled with the Holy Spirit before he was baptized.

The text reads, "So Ananias departed and entered the house. And laying his hands on him he said, 'Brother Saul, the Lord Jesus who appeared to you on the road by which you came has sent me so that you may regain your sight and be filled with the Holy Spirit.'
And immediately something like scales fell from his eyes, and he regained his sight. Then he rose and was baptized; and taking food, he was strengthened."

In 1 Corinthians 1:16–17, Paul writes, "I did baptize also the household of Stephanas. Beyond that, I do not know whether I baptized anyone else. For Christ did not send me to baptize but to preach the Gospel, and not with words of eloquent wisdom, lest the cross of Christ be emptied of its power."

Here we read that Paul was sent by God to preach the gospel and not to baptize. This shows us that baptism is something different from the gospel. If baptism is part of the gospel, then why divide the two in such a clear way?

Notice that at the end of verse 16, Paul writes, "I don't remember if I baptized anyone else." This statement becomes a rather humorous one when read in the light of baptismal regeneration teaching. It is hard to imagine Paul believing that one has to be baptized in order to be saved while at the same time saying he does not remember everyone whom he baptized in Corinth.

To this, we can add the thief on the cross, whom we saw earlier. He was saved while hanging on the cross, and so of course he was never baptized.

If you talk to someone who says that one must be baptized in order to be saved and want to get to the heart of the matter, try asking the following question. "Let's say that we have someone who believes in the gospel. Not just head knowledge, but true faith. That person really believes the gospel. And that person wants to be baptized, truly, from the heart. But the person dies before he or she is baptized. Where does that person go? To Heaven or Hell?"

Either way one answers the question, baptismal regeneration is shown to be untrue. If the answer to the question is, "Heaven," then baptism does not save; the person was saved before he or she was baptized. But if the answer to the question is "Hell," then baptismal regeneration is shown to be a system of works—righteousness, as the person in the example was not saved by faith alone in Jesus Christ. As we have seen earlier, you cannot obtain salvation by good works. No matter which way you look at it, the Bible teaches that women and men are saved by faith, not by being baptized.

One could answer, "I don't know what happens; God is their judge." But this is being disingenuous. If one teaches that baptism is essential for salvation, then one must be consistent and say that if you believe the gospel but die before you are baptized, then you go to Hell. If something is essential, then it is essential, period.

If it is not essential, then we have the teaching of two different gospels at the same time. Yet, the Bible teaches that there is only one true gospel, and it is a gospel of grace.[13]

---

[13] "I am astonished that you are so quickly deserting him who called you in the grace of Christ and are turning to a different gospel—not that there is another one, but there are some who trouble you and want to distort the gospel of Christ. But even if we or an angel from heaven should preach to you a gospel contrary to the one we preached to you, let him be accursed. As we have said before, so now I say again: If anyone is preaching to you a gospel contrary to the one you received, let him be accursed" (Galatians 1:6–9).

B

WHAT ABOUT JAMES, CHAPTER TWO?

James writes in James 2:24–26, "You see that a person is justified by works and not by faith alone. And in the same way was not also Rahab the prostitute justified by works when she received the messengers and sent them out by another way? For as the body apart from the spirit is dead, so also faith apart from works is dead."

Paul writes in Ephesians 2:8–9, "For by grace you have been saved through faith. And this is not your own doing; it is the gift of God, not a result of works, so that no one may boast."

Do these two passages contradict each other? No, they don't at all. Without contradiction, the Bible teaches that you are saved only by God's grace and not by any number or type of good works or religious rituals.

Here are three possible interpretations of the Scripture from James.

1. James is talking about people being justified, or being righteous in the sight of other people. In verses 15–16, the justification is of the richer believer in the eyes of the poorer. With Abraham (v. 20–24), in Genesis 15:6 it says, "...he believed the Lord, and he counted it to him as righteousness."

Abraham was already a believer when asked by God to sacrifice his son Isaac in Genesis 22. When he was going to go through with the act, this showed that his faith was real. Abraham was justified before God through his obedience. But Abraham's obedience and justification came after he already had faith.

In a similar way, Rahab was justified in the eyes of the messengers she saved. Before this, she already had faith in the one true God; now she was acting out from her faith. It's not that she suddenly came to know the Lord when she helped the Jews; that's putting the cart before the horse. First, she believed in God, then because of that faith, she acted.

2. James is saying that when one is saved by faith (belief) alone in the life, death, and bodily resurrection of Jesus Christ, he is saved by a faith that will produce good deeds and changes in the person's life. He is talking about a lifestyle, not about doing specific works in order to be saved.

For Paul as for James, the key issue is the kind of faith or trust we have in God. Paul writes that a true faith in God will save. James writes that a true faith in God will produce good works. We are looking at two sides of the same faith.

The instant any person is saved freely by God's grace through faith, many things happen. Of them, one is that the person is "born again" (John 3:3, 3:5–7). Another is that person is made into a "new creation" (2 Corinthians 5:17). A third is that the person has the Holy Spirit living inside of him or her (Romans 8:9–11; Colossians 2:9–10), who is sanctifying him or her (Romans 15:16; 1 Thessalonians 5:23–24). With all of this happening, how can this person not produce good deeds? By deeds, I mean changes in their character, lifestyle, actions, and heart that take place over time at different rates for different people.

In the Parable of the Sower, Jesus said that the believer is "the one who hears the word and understands it. He indeed bears fruit and yields, in one case a hundredfold, in another sixty, and in another thirty" (Matthew 13:23).

We should all be bearing fruit for the Lord, some more, some less. Jesus didn't condemn the person who brought forth thirty and shame him for not producing the same as the one who made one hundred. No, it's all good as we work for the Kingdom. You produce some fruit, I produce some fruit, and God is glorified by our efforts.

Take as another example the Parable of the Talents (Luke 19:11–27). Though each person started with the same number of minas, one person made ten more minas and another made five minas. Did the king in the parable get mad at the person who made five? Not at all. He was happy and gave that person responsibility equal to the minas that he had made.

We don't need to all be producing the same amount of fruit, but we should be producing fruit—which blesses others and is used by God to change lives for Him.

3. The person who claims to have true faith really doesn't believe in God. All they are doing is claiming to have faith, but it's a sham. Anyone can claim to be a Christian, but God truly knows those who are His and truly have faith in Christ.

In certain verses in this passage, James is describing a faith that can never save. It is not true faith. This is seen in verses 14 and 19. Verse 19 is very clear. James writes that even the demons have faith, but it is not saving faith. They believe that there is one God, but they do not trust in this one God for salvation.

James is not saying that the demons have faith or trust in God for salvation, but that they aren't saved because they do not have any works.

James is saying that their faith is a mere intellectual assent that there is one God; yet, their recognition of God is without trust in Him for salvation. This is before works ever come into the picture. Their lack of true faith is the thing that keeps them from being saved. Their works (evil) only show what kind of "faith" in God they have—a recognition that God exists, but not that they are trusting in Him for salvation.

In each case, it's the person's or being's faith that determines what action he or she will take. Abraham and Rahab believed in God, and therefore they were obedient to Him. Demons do not believe in God, and therefore they do not do good works for God's glory.

Further, James 2:26 says, "...faith without deeds is dead." Notice that James writes "deeds" in the plural. If he wanted to say that this means that you had to do good works in order to receive salvation, the questions must be asked, "What deeds do I need to do in order to be saved?" "How often would I have to do them?" "How would I know that these deeds are the right ones?" James does not address these questions. If they were viable, it would mean that no one would ever be able to have assurance of his or her salvation.

And yet, the Bible teaches that we can know that we are saved.

1 John 5:12–13 says, "Whoever has the Son has life....I write these things to you who believe in the name of the Son of God that you may know that you have eternal life."

John 5:24 says, "Truly, truly, I say to you, whoever hears my word and believes him who sent me has eternal life. He does not come into judgment, but has passed from death to life."

When you look at the big picture, it's humorous to think that by giving a few extra dollars to a church, or by reading an extra chapter of the Bible, or by witnessing to a certain number of people, etc., that we are suddenly going to equal the standard that God has set for having a relationship with Him. This standard is 100 percent total and complete perfection in all that we say, think, and do.

Can we really think that by giving an extra couple of bucks to church that we are going to gain a relationship with the perfect, eternal, Creator, the God of the universe?

Do we imagine that a little extra Bible reading will give us a perfect standing before a perfect God? This is impossible. God's commandments are to show unbelievers their sinful state before a holy God and their need of a Savior. And they are also to guide believers in how to live for Him after receiving salvation.

C

DOES PURGATORY EXIST?

It is claimed that there is a place that lies between earth and Heaven called Purgatory.

In looking at the existence of Purgatory, I'm not out to "Catholic bash," but the subject should be included in a book that deals with the full sufficiency of Christ's death and bodily resurrection as full payment for our sins.

If you are Catholic, please be encouraged by what the Bible says concerning life after death for any believer in Christ. God does not want for you to worry about Purgatory, but rather rejoice that an immediate entrance into the presence of God awaits everyone who believes in the Gospel.

First, let's look at what Purgatory is and what it is not.

From the Compendium of the Catechism of the Catholic Church:

> 210. What is purgatory?
>
> Purgatory is the state of those who die in God's friendship, assured of their eternal salvation, but who still have need of purification to enter into the happiness of heaven.
>
> 211. How can we help the souls being purified in purgatory?
>
> Because of the communion of saints, the faithful who are still pilgrims on earth are able to help the souls in purgatory by offering prayers in suffrage for them, especially the Eucharistic sacrifice. They also help them by almsgiving, indulgences, and works of penance.[14]

From the website, "Catechism of the Catholic Church":

> III. THE FINAL PURIFICATION, OR PURGATORY
>
> 1030. All who die in God's grace and friendship, but

---

[14] "What is Purgatory?" *Compendium of the Catechism of the Catholic Church* (Vatican City: Libreria Editrice Vaticana, 2005): http://www.vatican.va/archive/compendium_ccc/documents/archive_2005_compendium-ccc_en.html#I%20Believe%20in%20the%20Holy%20Spirit

still imperfectly purified, are indeed assured of their eternal salvation; but after death, they undergo purification, so as to achieve the holiness necessary to enter the joy of heaven.

1031. The Church gives the name Purgatory to this final purification of the elect, which is entirely different from the punishment of the damned.

It also refers to Purgatory as "a purifying fire" and "a cleansing fire."[15]

It is wrong to say that some who go to Purgatory then go to Hell. This is not true. According to Catholic teaching, all those who go to Purgatory will eventually go to Heaven. But according to the Bible, does such a place exist?

First, as we've seen throughout this book, Christ's death and resurrection is sufficient to pay for all of our sins.

His sacrifice for our sins was complete and final. Take for example the following verses from the Book of Hebrews.

Hebrews 9:26b says, "...he has appeared once for all at the end of the ages to put away sin by the sacrifice of himself."

Hebrews 10:11–12 reads, "And every priest stands daily at his service, offering repeatedly the same sacrifices, which can never take away sins. But when Christ had offered for all time a single sacrifice for sins, he sat down at the right hand of God."

Hebrews 10:17–18 says, "I will remember their sins and their lawless deeds no more." Where there is forgiveness of these, there is no longer any offering for sin."

You can see the tone of finality and completeness here.

Christ was our one, only, and complete sacrifice for our sins. We do not need to add to that sacrifice through suffering or purification in Purgatory.

1 Corinthians 5:7b says, "Christ, our Passover lamb, has been sacrificed."

That's it. Nothing more is needed.

On the cross, Jesus said, "It is finished!" (John 19:30).

---

[15] "The Final Purification, or Purgatory," *Compendium of the Catechism of the Catholic Church* (Vatican City: Libreria Editrice Vaticana, 2005): http://www.vatican.va/archive/ccc_css/archive/catechism/p123a12.htm

The Bible teaches that one is instantly made perfect by Jesus Christ upon death. We don't need to suffer in Purgatory because Christ suffered for us. That's the good news of the gospel. Jesus did all of the suffering. All of the punishment for our sins was placed upon Christ. Not one-half, two-thirds, or three-fourths of the punishment and suffering, but all of it.

Isaiah 53:5–6 says, "But he was pierced for our transgressions; he was crushed for our iniquities; upon him was the chastisement that brought us peace, and with his wounds we are healed. All we like sheep have gone astray; we have turned—every one—to his own way; and the Lord has laid on him the iniquity of us all."

There is no clear or specific mention of Purgatory in the New Testament. In contrast, whenever we see believers in Scripture who die, they always go immediately to Paradise. Take as examples both the thief on the cross and Lazarus.

In Luke 23:42–43, the thief said to Jesus, "'Jesus, remember me when you come into your kingdom.' And he said to him, 'Truly, I say to you, today you will be with me in Paradise.'"

The thief would be with Jesus not after being purified for the rest of his sins, but immediately, that day, he would be with Jesus in Paradise. He didn't do anything for God and God's Kingdom, and yet he was taken directly into paradise to be with the Lord Jesus and other believers forever.

Looking at the Greek word for "paradise," we do not find any teaching or hints of a need for purification from sins.

The Greek for "paradise" is "paradises," and Mounce defines it as, "a park, a forest where wild beasts were kept for hunting; a pleasure-park, a garden of trees of various kinds; used in the LXX [Septuagint—the Greek translation of the Old Testament] for the Garden of Eden."[16]

This was a good place, my friends. This is Heaven as good as it can be before the restoration of the earth and the entire universe.

There is no pain here, no act of purification, and there is no need for it, for Christ did that on the cross. When Jesus died on the cross and rose bodily from the grave, He didn't just pay for some of our sins, He paid the price in full for all of them. The deal is done.

The second example is Lazarus, from the story of the rich man and Lazarus, which we looked at in chapter eight.

---

[16] William D. Mounce, *Mounce's Complete Expository Dictionary of Old & New Testament Words* (Grand Rapids: Zondervan, 2006): 1233.

Lazarus died and "was carried by the angels to Abraham's side" or "bosom," where he was "comforted." There is no mention of his being purified.

Albert Barnes's *Notes on the Bible* says in regards to the meaning of the words "Abraham's side" (*Abraam kolpos*), "This is a phrase taken from the practice of reclining at meals, where the head of one lay on the bosom of another, and the phrase, therefore, denotes intimacy and friendship....The Jews had no doubt that Abraham was in paradise. To say that Lazarus was in his bosom was, therefore, the same as to say that he was admitted to heaven and made happy there."[17] (e-Sword).

Here are some other supporting Scriptures that show that believers immediately go to be with God when they die.

In 2 Corinthians 5:8, Paul writes, "Yes, we are of good courage, and we would rather be away from the body and at home with the Lord."

No other options are given, either living on earth "in the body" or with God "at home with the Lord."

Similarly, Paul writes in Philippians 1:21–23, "For to me to live is Christ, and to die is gain. If I am to live in the flesh, that means fruitful labor for me. Yet which I shall choose I cannot tell. I am hard pressed between the two. My desire is to depart and be with Christ, for that is far better."

We see no mention of Purgatory. Paul writes simply, "Depart and be with Christ."

1 Corinthians 15:51–52 says, "I tell you a mystery. We shall not all sleep, but we shall all be changed, in a moment, in the twinkling of an eye, at the last trumpet. For the trumpet will sound, and the dead will be raised imperishable, and we shall be changed."

Here too there is no mention of Purgatory. The dead will be "raised imperishable," and those who are alive at that time will be instantly changed and ready to be with God.

1 Thessalonians 4:16–18 reads, "For the Lord himself will descend from heaven with a cry of command, with the voice of an archangel, and with the sound of the trumpet of God. And the dead in Christ will rise first. Then we who are alive, who are left, will be caught up together with them in the clouds to meet the Lord in the air, and so we will always be with the Lord. Therefore encourage one another with these words."

---

[17] Accessed through E-Sword program (www.e-sword.net/index.html).

The dead rise, others go to meet the Lord, and then both groups (all believers) will always be with the Lord.

No mention of Purgatory. And Paul wants his readers/listeners to be encouraged by these words.

Psalm 103:12, 2-3a say, "As far as the east is from the west, so far does he remove our transgressions from us...Bless the Lord, O my soul, and forget not all his benefits, who forgives all your iniquity."

D

POEM – THE THIEF ON THE CROSS

I have committed adultery. Dozens of times over.
I have told one hundred lies. I don't know where the truth ends and the lies begin.
Jesus, remember me when you come into your kingdom.

I have kept the poor, poor. And gave unfair advantage to the rich.
I have envied the rich and poor alike. To the point where my blood turned green.
Jesus, remember me when you come into your kingdom.

I have boasted and bragged. And deliberately put my interests before others.
I have exalted myself at the expense of others.
Jesus, remember me when you come into your kingdom.

I have killed many times over. My hands are stained with blood.
I have murdered the innocent. I paid no heed to their cries.
Jesus, remember me when you come into your kingdom.

I have cheated and stolen my way. To a warehouse full of items.
I have taken when I was not in need. All for my hands alone.
Jesus, remember me when you come into your kingdom.

I have cared not for God and His ways. I have done as I pleased.
I have used religion to my advantage. I was a wolf in sheep's clothing.

Who am I?

I am you.
I am me.
I am every person.

With that, we are introduced to humanity.
With that, we are introduced to the thief on the cross.

By Christopher Hearn

E

POEM – JESUS IS ALWAYS WITH ME

Jesus is always with me.

In the morning when I wake, His sun shines to greet me.
Through the day He is here.
From the rain that refreshes and brings life, to the fog that cools, and
wraps the gentle works of His hands like a present.
When His sun sets He is with me with the colors of the sky.
He creates His work.
Slowly, carefully never rushed.
Until the crescendo comes, and the canvas begins to slowly fade.
But even then, Jesus is with me.
I look up to the lights, each one unique with its own distinct touch from
the Master.
When I look up and see nothing, Jesus sends a gentle breeze to remind me.

He has not forgotten.

By Christopher Hearn

ABOUT THE AUTHOR

Christopher Hearn has served as a missionary to Russia with Operation Mobilization (OM) and currently is the Pastor of the First Baptist Church of New Sweden, Maine. He has a MDIV from Bethel Theological Seminary San Diego.